The Wrong Cat

BOOKS BY LORNA CROZIER

POETRY

Inside Is the Sky (1976)

Crow's Black Joy (1979)

Humans and Other Beasts (1980)

No Longer Two People (with Patrick Lane) (1981)

The Weather (1983)

The Garden Going On Without Us (1985)

Angels of Flesh, Angels of Silence (1988)

Inventing the Hawk (1992)

Everything Arrives at the Light (1995)

A Saving Grace (1996)

What the Living Won't Let Go (1999)

Apocrypha of Light (2002)

Bones in Their Wings: Ghazals (2003)

Whetstone (2005)

The Blue Hour of the Day: Selected Poems (2007)

Small Mechanics (2011)

The Wrong Cat (2015)

NON-FICTION

Small Beneath the Sky (2009)

The Book of Marvels: A Compendium of Everyday Things (2012)

ANTHOLOGIES

A Sudden Radiance (with Gary Hyland) (1987)

Breathing Fire (with Patrick Lane) (1995)

Desire in Seven Voices (2000)

Addicted: Notes from the Belly of the Beast (with Patrick Lane) (2001)

Breathing Fire 2 (with Patrick Lane) (2004)

Best Canadian Poetry 2010 (2010)

The Wrong Cat

poems

LORNA CROZIER

McCLELLAND & STEWART

Library and Archives of Canada Cataloguing in Publication
available upon request.

ISBN: 978-0-7710-2391-0
ebook ISBN: 978-0-7710-2392-7

Published simultaneously in the United States of America
by McClelland & Stewart, a division of Random House of Canada Limited,
a Penguin Random House Company

Library of Congress Control Number: 2014920837

Typeset in Dante by Sean Tai
Printed and bound in USA

McClelland & Stewart,
a division of Random House of Canada Limited,
a Penguin Random House Company
www.penguinrandomhouse.ca

1 2 3 4 5   19 18 17 16 15

Penguin
Random
House

For Barry and Linda Crozier

I lean forward because I almost have it and don't.
Do you know the wild horse poem?
The sound of unshod hooves on desert grass, running?

PATRICK LANE, "LISTEN" FROM *WASHITA*

CONTENTS

III

IV

The Wrong Cat

I

Unlike the dog,
its opposite,
a cat defies
the anecdotal,
goes for the lyric,
music made from
bone and muscle
and the grace
notes
of paws.

BARREN

In the orchard a deer stands on his hind legs.
Out early for a walk, before the village stirs,
she hopes he's come for her, his chest
white with moon-spill, his antlers tall
hard hands, fingers splayed. They touch
the high things humans don't sense are there.
His eyes have dimmed; he's weary
from his travels through the deadfall,
the fallow fields, the raised meadow
of little heartbeats. When he gets close to her,
moving with a shaman's roll from foot to foot,
will he place his mouth upon her mouth
and blow the found one in?

TELLING WHAT FUTURE

Colville's crow wakes me
at 3 a.m. Silent for too long
he's like my heart
breaking from a stupor,
in his gut the tongues
of naked birds.

High in the spruce
outside my window
he cries his never-song,
tries to second-guess
what moves
or doesn't move below.

Black blur of grief
to come, death wish,
teach me to go into darkness
with so much noise.

BOOK OF SMALL MISTAKES

Her supervisor agrees it's worth the years of study,
worthy of the grants. She starts with her husband:
he leaves crumbs on the breadboard every morning,
doesn't tighten the cap on the toothpaste tube,
doesn't replace the toilet paper when it runs out.
Is it a small mistake that he never learns
from her corrections? A small mistake that all
her whites turned pink when he tossed his red
sweatshirt in the wash? Meanwhile, there are the mice.
All their slips are small, depending on how she chooses
to use the word. Their rice-sized droppings on cookie tins,
their tooth marks in the beeswax candles in the drawer.
Her husband says she reminds him of a mouse with all her
    scratchings,
observing him at breakfast over toast, then making notes
as if she were not mouse but mole, one who'd infiltrated
their marriage years ago. A small mistake should be
the size of the button on a cuff, the toe of a tree frog,
black mosquito larvae, the hair on a chin.
Soon she's so busy with her book she forgets his birthday,
forgets to put the chicken in the oven, forgets to sleep or go
to work in the bakery she once owned. As you'd expect
he stays on the jobsite longer. In the *Book of Small Mistakes,*
a small mistake, she writes for her defence,
should be the size of a screw that holds the hands
of a watch together, the size of a spot before it becomes
a melanoma, the size of one eyelet
in a child's white shoe
she never had the chance
to lace and tie.

LATER THEY'LL SAY SHE GOT LOST IN THE BLIZZARD

Duped by the moon
a woman walks into snow and knows
at once what she once was.
Feathers return to the hollow
above her shoulder blades,
gravity swoops from the earth
into the sky
and she soars upward,
head turning like an owl's,
eyes big enough
to see a vole
sleeping in its soft
sarcophagus of snow;
when she swerves
to look at what's behind
she glimpses
through the farmhouse window
her daughter, her white-haired
husband and the old
amnesiac who is her father
dumbly waiting at the table
she had set,
their empty plates
shining from this height
as if the moon itself
had been sliced like a winter turnip
and could serve no better purpose
than to hold what they would eat.

VAN GOGH WENT OUT TO PAINT THE STARS

Needing a religion, you go out to paint
the fireflies. Back inside, under the lamp,
you see the lumen on the canvas
isn't from the embers of insects
but from the face of Jesus, his sad eyes.

Remember the woman who found his visage
in oatmeal burping on the stove? The man who saved
the all-dressed pizza delivered to his door
and charged everyone ten bucks to see,
among the anchovies, the crucifixion.

We've been told God's in everything.
Here's the proof. Even if you're looking
for something else, there's a likelihood,
if you live in middle North America – rural,
small town – you'll find him. At least a part.
His anguished foot in the wine stain
on your carpet, his heart on your flannel sleeve.

And pilgrims will come to you from Gull Lake,
from Rosetown, from Minneota;
they'll leave their crutches on your stairs,
quibble about the price then eat you
out of house and lettuce patch until they're healed.
Better to have captured flying bioluminescent bugs
in a jar and let them go. The trouble's your taste

for theophany, your obdurate desire to find
a meaning other than what's here.

You see redemption in the ragged
footfalls of the rain. Like St. Teresa of Ávila
you see the lord in pots and pans
and forget the good they do as simply
pots and pans in someone's kitchen.
Sometimes a starry, starry night is just
a night with stars.

THE BEGINNING OF ABSTRACTIONS

Some time ago, the old ones say,
four moons hung above the garden
every solstice, that is, the moon in all its phases
all at once. Imagine the beauty of it,
every creature, every blossom washed in blue.

When that happened, a woman was to lie
in the meadow, knees open so the full
moon's seeds would steal inside her.

If she turned to the new moon – completely dark –
what its seeds would ripen into
was not flesh but intellect, a boneless,
breathless baby made of numbers,
secret signs, and signatures,
a baby that would give you
nothing back.

Raindrops shivered as they touched
her face, her womb heavy
with abstractions, with *pi,* prime,
the difference between the *absolute* and *nothing;*
meanwhile the deer and so on, especially
the field mice gathering the grains
the quarter moons left behind.

THE MASK

She kept the mask, not knowing
what to do with it. That hard plastic skin
moulded to the shape of his face, fitted over
his head and attached to the treatment table.
It sits in a coffee-maker box
on the closet shelf above the shoes
she's kept as well, though all the clothes
are gone. She tells no one. It's been three years –
her friends and son wouldn't understand.

Tonight she drops his shoes in a garbage bag,
relaxes her gaze, something she's learned
to do in yoga so she doesn't really see.
Then she takes down the box that promises
Maximum Capacity, Brew Strength Control,
Easy-to-Fill Water Reservoir.

She opens the lid: there it is, his face –
an empty husk, cut-outs for the mouth and nose,
none for the eyes. When asked if he wanted them,
he'd said no. She thought he'd made that choice
so he wouldn't see the blank expression
of the radiographer, the cold machine
that promised nothing. Later she wondered if,
in some strange way, he was getting ready.
Not only lying still but blind now too,
the table sliding him headfirst into a fire.

He'd practised death so well,
when she brought him home, she kept checking
with a feather pulled from a pillow.
In the choir, he'd learned to turn a single breath
into so much sound it filled their church.
It undermined the light.

More than any photograph taken near the last,
the cast holds his likeness. She runs her fingers over
his nose, the shells of his ears, his jaw's parentheses.
What disturbs her most is the mouth, the hope-
lessness of the opening his lips surround.

She lies down on what she calls *their* bed
and dons the mask. It doesn't fit, of course,
her face is small inside it. Three years.
She trembles under the duvet that must be
stuffed with snow. Her eyes won't open.
She doesn't know how to end what she's begun.

NOTES FOR A SMALL POCKET

Dog of Morning

Morning – a wet-nosed dog
with flapping dewlaps –
rolls in a bed of basil
large as lettuce leaves
then shakes the scent all over us!

On such a day our lives
laugh out loud.

Missing You

In the desert country
of my childhood
the trees' roots
smell the water.

You are rain to me
where no rain falls.

Spider

So what if there's no
money in our wallets.
How joyous the spider is
though her eight feet
have no shoes.

Grief

So many are writing elegies
these days, to cranes, orcas,
long nights of snow, the archaic
courtesies of childhood, mice
in cupboards.

It's possible
to pine for anything –
good or bad –
when it's gone.

Missing You 2

To stop griping
I eat with the wooden spoon
clenched
between Dostoevsky's teeth
to keep him
from biting off his tongue.

Ars Poetica

Cezanne missed
his mother's funeral –
he wouldn't give up
a day of painting.

His teeth turned black,
not from punishment
but from licking
the tips of his brushes
to a point

so he could outline –
among many things –
the bather's toes.

Game

By the pond at night
three raccoons play
paper, scissors, rock.
They have the hands
to do it. When they get bored
they turn ahead the clocks
while you lie sleeping.
That's why, no matter
what your age, by dawn
your time is up.

Call and Response

The moth's single thought
is light. Is that enough philosophy
to get by on? Wings and all
thrumming the bulb, the moth
replies, *Dunno, dunno, dunno.*

Missing You 3

At noon the sky is cloudless:
wind has herded its wild horses
out of sight.

Now they're in their pastures
far to the east.

Do you hear the rattle
of oats in the pail?
It's a countrywoman
calling down the rain.

Listen

You hate the undertaker
faces of the lilies
but there's more death
in the peony's big blooms;
you hear each petal
as it falls.

Humility

Today the world
turns hermit,
finds a hut to go to,
a creek of sadness,
a crooked tree.

SIXTY-SIX WINTERS

A prairie road in winter. Is this what heaven's like?
Long, flat, and open, its sheen sheering your eyes?
All is white but a white of many colours

except for the grackle come back too soon.
He drops from the fence, rises and drops again,
smitten with his tracks. Snow sparks

underfoot, everything's high voltage.
Wind comes at you from four directions,
the sound entirely its own, no leaves to rattle,

nothing on the line, no opening unclosed.
Your hips can barely carry you, too heavy
with the past. It hunches in the swirl ahead,

wolf-like, frost-furred, without a shadow.
When you bury your face in its neck,
will it be your mother? You would give

the years you have ahead of you
to be so eaten, to die inside
her snowy belly as you once lived.

AN EXTRAORDINARY FONDNESS FOR BEETLES

I like to think of my soul
taking on the shape of a beetle,
that is, the many shapes of what it means
to be a beetle since there are over
360,000 species of its kind.

There's the Japanese, silver and flat
as a dime so it can slip under
the thinnest detritus on the ground.
And the clicking beetle. Like someone cool
from the '50s, snapping his fingers to Miles,
it flips into the air without twitching a wing.

As a beetle, the soul will do
what I can't do now:
excrete wax to keep in moisture,
turn its legs into stilts to raise itself
above burning tar or sand,
drum its belly on the ground
so it's called the abdomen-talking beetle.
Imagine the abdomen-talking soul!

It can strip flesh off a saint
or a bull elk or a whale, take out a whole
cotton crop and forest or, more modestly,
ruin a bag of flour. It can roll dung as if it were
a dogged Dinky tractor chosen to shove the sun
from one galaxy to the next. I like to think
of my soul as that beetle, pushing what's left
of the light that once was me
out of the world.

I I

The inventor of the shutter
and light-filter mechanism
had been watching the pupils of his cat.
Every photograph has a parallel
a cat has taken – without a touch
of sentiment, a perfect
composition of the never-seen
and shadow.

REWILDING

Wanted an edge, he said, something in the forest
to ignite his fear. When he came upon a fallen deer,
he hefted it onto his back and lugged it for miles
along the trail. To his surprise his muscles knew
how to carry a kill, their grace and power buried
in his genes. He used the world *primeval*, said
halfway to the cabin, he even yelled and kept on
yelling. Scared his friend – "Put it down" –
but he went on, a bent-over trot across the twigs
and needles, the head hanging over his head,
a transformation hat, flies spilling down his face,
he spat them out like sour berries. Back home,
what he did to her in bed – he didn't want to
bathe – wasn't making love but she didn't care.
On all fours, she was long and lean; thighs and biceps
too, found something from the past she'd lost.
It was like the first time they'd slept together
and the year before the child. Two nights earlier
someone had kicked three pickets
in the fence around the house and broken them in half.
It happened again. She woke to find him
crouched in the porch, naked in the dark,
looking out, a baseball bat in his hand. "Still hunter,"
he said, she knew he liked the sound of it,
"let him come to me." Back in bed when he slept again
he ground his teeth, his legs panicked like a dog's.
He called it rewilding and claimed it was a movement.
Bears and wolves let loose in English countrysides,
cougars lowered in nets to the mountains, rattlesnakes
dropped in the drylands where they could nest. To her

it was the crack of wood on bone, the heat of his mouth
moving slowly up her legs, the feral muscles
carrying across the black plains of the past
the rotten kill to her door.

ONCE THERE WAS A SINGING

A blackbird bit her tongue.
That's what started the singing
though she couldn't sing
before. She was the one, not Orpheus,
the animals walked into the sun
to listen to, the voice Ulysses
made so much of, the crew strapping him
to the mast – you've heard all this before.

Now the animals, half starved,
quivering, won't leave their lairs.
The cities close in on them, devour
the meadows, the groves, the marshes.
Trees turn into ghosts and won't grow leaves.

The new Ulysses is the coxswain
on the rowing team. His shouts echo
and re-echo across the lake
where children splash behind the ropes.
Their mothers stand like bitterns in the water,
necks stretched, eyes hard and glazed.

Rick-rick-rick is what they hear
when she starts singing. After –
you've heard all this before, you're undismayed –
her mouth falls open and she drools.

PITY POOR MAN UNKIND NOT

Pity the poor earthworm who, split in two,
for a time survives, one part half dead and half alive,
the other, the opposite. Whatever you believe
it misses itself, entirely. Pity the guard dog who isn't
allowed to love. It takes the strength of all its bared teeth
to stop its tail from wagging. Pity the left-handed man who sees
only with his left eye but who leans in everything to the right.
Pity the poor cockroach with its thirteen-chambered heart
and no one, not even weevils, tics, and flies, gives a hoot.
Pity, oh pity, the poor one inside me, the child no one sings to,
the sister drowned in the womb, the lonely drunken
father no one leads back home. Pity that poor unkind me
who sits by an ugly phone that won't fit in a pocket,
who's waited since the '60s for it to ring. "Hello, pity,"
I say to no one on the line. "Take a taxi over
and I'll pay."

LIKE A BODY FALLING

Ravens pull the bell ropes of the rain.
Thunder from far off sounds like a body
falling through the seven spheres of light.

The feet of the last angel to land on the earth
were black, blacker still after he strode through
the library at Alexandria, ankle-high in soot and ashes,
assured the wisdom gathered before the reign
of Yahweh had been burned away.

Before the resurrection, the clouds looked unambitious,
unperplexed. Some, though, were fashioned
from the beard of Moses before it thinned;
others took on the darkness of Sarah's afterbirth,
blue-black. She was ninety when she bore a son.

When the timpani of thunder stops,
the sky's so clear it's as if the storm didn't happen.
The ravens lose their grip. Frogs, not a plague,
but dozens bright as brass, startle the girl who runs
barefoot through the grass. They are the size
of the big screws in a drum kit.

NOT TROUBLED BY HER BREATH

Held by the hand of God –
not what she is but the small thing

she once was. A wood mouse,
a cow's eye, a leaf chameleon.

Touched is what they call the crazy.
Standing on two legs

doesn't feel good to her,
comfort doesn't feel good to her.

She chops a hole in the ice,
then stretches out,

face suspended above the cold
so her spirit can reach down

to what looks up
from that dark water.

COMPENDIUM ON CROWS

Brains so sharp they know everything at once
and don't sort it into parts, their caw, caw, caw
parsed only by the dead in the stench of the gut.

Two crows or one: sorrow and joy have nothing
to do with them. Meat does, and the eyes of lambs,
and rotting matter. In the high boughs of the spruce

they tuck their feet beneath their robes and take confession.
Go on – it's you who gives them that, their black
Madonnas, their worry beads of bones.

They have no gods of punishment or absolution.
They have no stations. Yet, without exception,
they dote on their young, give them what they lack,

pluck the songbird's newly hatched like living plums.

OTTER

The river otter spotted on the lawn at twilight
was only passing through, they thought, their faith
in fences and the closeness of the creek a block
or so away. When morning broke, the backyard pond
was stripped of lilies, marsh marigolds, and rushes.
At the water's edge, a creamsicle turned out to be
the head of the shubunkin who'd been with them
fifteen years. Two nights later the otter killed the others,
the koi they called The Golden One, the black moors,
the humpback carp. The wildlife officer confirmed their fears.
When the fish ran out, the otter would crack the turtles open,
the smaller female first, then the next, wider than a dinner plate.
A live trap, he told them, wouldn't work. Otters were too smart
for that. No, he wouldn't use a leg-hold; he'd set a baited cage
in the pond, the door would drop, and the otter die by drowning.
We'll get back to you, they said. After the second raid,
they'd been so angry, so bereaved, they'd talked of ways:
rat poison – they had some in the shed – a rifle and a jacklight
though someone on the street was likely to complain.
"I've never killed a living thing," she said, "not deliberately
at least, except for insects." The would-be murderer she'd become
was as shocking as her tibia meeting the air the time
her leg fractured. "That's because you were a girl," he said.
Every boy he knew had a BB gun, a slingshot, and they'd used them.
They walked around the fences, filled in the gaps, he built
another gate. The otter tunnelled under. They dug a trench
and poured cement. That night they listened for the barking
of the neighbour's dog, wished the turtles could cry out.
The trapper said the otter would thrash in the cage, it could take
a while, the claws might rip the lining. Who could bear it?

Months before, through the bedroom's sliding doors,
she'd seen an otter reclining on the front deck.
Longer than the average man and lush –
could it see her through the glass? – its life force
so intense light quilled and quivered all around it.
Fleshy but not an ounce of wasted flesh – surely it was
female, this liquid creature, gleaming as if just risen
from a bath and, indolent and vain, was posing for a painter
or waiting for a slave to fetch some herring roe, some towels
of Turkish cotton. How extravagant and human this conceit.
Would things be better if she could see herself as otter?
Feel that blast in the blood that means a different way of being
deep inside, her body rising from a river, a sea-run fish
whipping in her grip, that shine on teeth and tongue
the pearly scales of steelhead.

HEART SUTRA

The bullet burned through his heart
but did not kill him. "He had no heart,"
the host said. What should have turned him
into merely meat and bones shot through the emptiness
inside. "Then what pumped his blood?" she asked,
she and her husband guests for the night
at the summer cabin two hours from town.
"His hate, his rage," their friend replied.
Whatever the truth of it, in the Reuters photos
he'd passed across the table, she could see
the healed-over hole on his chest like a thumbprint
pressed into dough and in another, the exit wound
that pouted below his left shoulder blade.
The hostess, who'd spent hours stirring at the stove
so she could serve the perfect risotto, said,
"The scars make him more attractive,"
as if they were chatting about a bad-boy
movie star, not a soldier on trial for rape,
as if he'd find redemption
in the arms of a woman who could cook.
The guest hated what began to burn inside her,
a loathing for the friends who'd invited them
to stay the night and some shameful dark
longing for this terrible stranger and his
phantom heart. She tried to think instead of the cicatrix
that slashed diagonally across her husband's breast,
just missing the nipple that was more
sensitive than hers, her teeth could tell you.
"A knife cut," he said when they first met,
"got it in a bar." Years later he confessed

as a kid he'd smashed into a barbed wire fence.
It was winter, snow climbed halfway up the posts,
the blood that shocked him into stillness
leapt from the gash, caught on the barbs,
and hardened into ice. Now, she swears,
every time they fuck she melts
one red bead, then another, in her mouth,
"Go, go, go," she whispers, "go beyond,
go thoroughly beyond," the heart sutra
précised by the Dalai Lama
a ghost pulse on her tongue.

MAN FROM ELSEWHERE

Man from Hades

You'd think he loved the dark,
But that's not right.
                    It's why
He brought me down, the red
Of pomegranate cut open
In my palm, its seeds
                    Of wet light.
I was my mother's child.
It was the farthest I could go
                    Without her.
I owe him that.
I owe him my love of solitude
And shamelessness.
                    I owe him
My ability to forget.

Man from Hades 2

No man tried harder to please me.
He pulled down clouds and geraniums,
He pulled down the stream where I used to bathe,
Gave me three hounds the colour of snow.
Their noses led them through the dark
And I didn't allow myself to wonder
What they fed on. And our marriage bed –
He did much to make me want
To lie there. The mattress smelled of every flower
I once loved. His own skin
Did not smell good to me. Was he dead,
This god of the dead? Was I dead too?
That would explain many things.
His throat had become the throat of a bird
Yet he could not sing.

Man from Hades 3

The daily tasks were different.
There was no sun
To make particular the dust
Or streak the windows.
There were no windows.
No wind, no rain or sickness,
No need of calendars or clocks.
But a marriage is a marriage
In whatever country. A man,
A man.

Man from the Promised Land

He was the north wind, the west,
And I very nearly blew away with him
My limbs light as grit. He whittled me,
Raised me to his lips and made me sing.
It was Arabic, it was Bedouin, Saskatchewan's
Great Sandhills, the Blackfoot and the Cree.
Oh, he was good to me. I shifted shape,
Moved as he moved, our tracks filled in.
Slow sift, was he, soft slide through fingers;
The dunes of hips and shoulder blades
Gilded by the sun. He raised me to his lips
And made me sing. The mouthpiece
Of my heart parched with grief.

Man from the Rain Forest

I thought I was done with him
But the rain brings back

The runnel of his fingers,
Their cool slide

Down my midriff,
Around my navel

And down again
Down.

The rain is labial, he said,
And showed me why.

Man from Eden

Oh, there was the apple, the nakedness –
That needs no telling. But before that
There were the animals, and I heard them all:
The secrets of the hare, the lizard's rasp,
The banter of bark and squawk and bird-lilt.
When I saw him in his skin and he saw me,
That talk turned into gibberish, and everything
They'd told me I forgot. He became my wolf,
My bullfrog, my feral cat, hawk on the updraft,
Sunlight filling my mouth, spider spinning her hunger
Across my breasts. Only he talked sense to me.
I thought that was what I needed. I thought too much.
Soon everything started to die. How lonely it is
In the garden. I look for him everywhere, I listen.
Is that him beneath the water, in the caught
Breath of bulrushes? In the bow, the viola
Of the cricket's wings?

Man from the Sargasso Sea

Surely he was once an eel, slick and run-on,
Writhing rainbow without colour,

Water-drenched. A wanderer who crossed
The seas and knew his way.

Mouth wide and dangerous.

I caught him with a torch
And a wooden boat.

I caught him with a net
My mother made me.

The next full tide I let him go.

Man from the Cariboo

He rode into the yard with five white horses,
And he in the middle on a big black,
His face burnt and chapped. I wanted
A horse more than a man, I told him that,
Bargained for a mare with legs like rifles
That fired when she galloped, and me
No more than wind on her withers.
Above me in my bed, sunlight rode the saddle
Of his long back. Nothing could break him
Though my touch, strong and sure as water,
Calmed the tremors, untied the knots,
Gentled his need to leave at the first
Call of dawn outside the window.
After he left, the mare wouldn't come near.
So white she is, she disappears in mist
Lifting from the grass, the breath
Of winter sleepers dreaming under drifts.
In the meadow, I wait for her to come to me
Without a rope or bridle, my hands
Offering her my hands.

Man from the North

He came out of the snow.
      Bones over his eyes
So he wouldn't go blind.

There was hunger and seal fat,
      The moon's marrow
Cracking in the sky.

We broke off flames
      From the frozen fire,
Sucked them

Till our mouths blistered:
      Wearing bones
On the outside of his body

Saved his sight,
But he saw death
      In every moving thing

And there was nothing
      I could do
To keep away the cold.

Man from the Stars

He comes home covered in a dust that shines.
Tells me he didn't know anybody's tongue.
When I undo his shirt I see he still has a body.
They're like us, he says, but they don't look up.
Though he doesn't smoke, every night I find him
In the darkness of the grove that blocks the sky,
A cigarette between his fingers, that little star.

Man from the Labyrinth

Where they got it wrong: they gave him virgins,
Terrified of course and weeping. What he wanted
Was a woman whose wisdom resides
In the sags and creases of the flesh. For a time
He rested his elegant head in my lap
And I found pleasure in his doorless manor,
His halls of no direction. But he wore me out
With his hide-and-seek and riddles, most
Not his own – What has four legs, etcetera.
He wanted to be a different kind of trouble.
Now they're back to virgins.
I'd warn them but what's the use. To stay alive
They'd have to choose to grow old.

Man from the East

It was his calligraphy, how he changed
With the merest touch the meaning of my body,
From wind to wing to heron, and lastly snow,
Snow an artist makes among the many colours
Simply by leaving the paper blank.

III

A cat sleeps
sixteen hours a day
because it's wearying
to own so much.
"In a cat's eyes
everything belongs to the cat,"
so the English proverb goes.

A COMMON LIFE

He didn't want her
when he was younger and now he does.
Claims his first affair, which made everything go wrong,
his fling with the flamenco dancer, was a big mistake.
The daughter of the hotel keeper in Barcelona, the man
who counted them among his foreign friends. Early evening
she saw them through the smeared glass of the greenhouse.
The girl in her red skirt straddled him on a chair.
What she remembers twenty years later is the skirt,
its flame and flare, how it looked as if their pale
torsos rose from the skins of large flayed animals
she'd weep for in her dreams. The mistake lasted three nights,
the girl crying on the platform as they, husband and wife,
caught the train, the second-class carriage, the toilet
bulb burnt out, their lovemaking ten years into their marriage
so tender she knew she'd be alone by Paris.
Now she's counting cormorant crucifixes on the rocks
in English Bay. Practising her Spanish, she says out loud,
Uno, dos, tres, cuatro. Ocho is the number she likes best,
its noisy ch in the centre, its perfect rhyme.
There were others – she'd heard it from their friends –
more as he got famous, the reps paid to pick him up,
a whirl of signings, single malts, and undone buttons,
dirty towels on bathroom floors. It was easy to fall
for his face, the same photo he'd used for years,
clipped white beard and hair, head bent,
eyelids half closed. His sensitivity and sorrow
beautifully posed. Now he's back. Yesterday he left
The Divine Comedy on her doorstep. Signed, as if he'd written it.
Later in the evening he phoned. Said every lover in his poems

was her, every loss, every happiness accounted for was her.
This morning, on her way home with groceries, she saw him
sitting in a car outside the house. She turned and walked back
the way she'd come, pushing into wind as if she pushed a cart
the two blocks to the ocean. If they'd stayed together, they'd be
grandparents now, they'd be sitting in the sun somewhere.
If they were lucky they'd be sweetly irked by one another.
They'd tell the stories of a common life. The truth is
she believes him, in some small place she knows he never left.
There were lovers after him, of course, three of them long-term,
one a husband, all of them now dead. She can't stop thinking
of their withered seeds inside her, dry and small as isotopes
shot into a prostate to make a tumour shrink.
Sometimes at night between the sheets she glows.
What she loves now is the cold coming in
off the ocean, there's no age to it, no countenance,
and the birds, three times three, *nueve,*
miming crosses as they dry their wings,
are not wounded, at least not that she can see.

JANUARY

Wind is not as fond of the aspens as it is in summer,
eyelids of leaves opening and closing with a breath,
yet the setting sun lingers on these greenless sticks
stuck upright in the snow. It tips and spills a wash of rose,
each tree in the grove flushed like skin from a bath,
the heat held minutes after. As she grows thin,
she likes the winter aspens more, not less, stands
among them in the cold, absorbs the dwindling gloam.
Thigh-deep in drifts, she raises her arms above her head
and sways. She has no kin on either side, in front, in back;
yet she joins them in their to-and-fro, their meanwhileness
and clatter, as she waits for the day's last light
to take her where it wants to go.

THE QUESTION

After they agreed to buy a new mattress, the one
they're lying on half the age of their marriage, she asks,
"Do you think it's true? That in any liaison one person
is more in love than the other?" He knows his answer's
crucial. How much time does he have?
"One, two, three," she's counting in the dark. He says,
"Isn't that like asking if you love one of your children more?"
"Since I don't have any, your question's moot."
Rhymes with shoot, he thinks. Feels like he's in a chute,
an about-to-be steer, his balls exposed. Wonders if the gun
in the drawer beside her – since he doesn't have a table,
his side crowded against the wall so he has to clamber over
the bottom of the bed or flop like a seal across her, fast asleep,
to pee at night, twice if he's lucky – wonders if the gun
is loaded. "Yes," he says, relieved she can't see his face,
"I believe it's true." Then a pause and, "I love you more."
"You think I'm a fool?" she says. "That I don't know you?"
Does he have a comeback? If this were a play,
she'd take out the gun and shoot him. He starts talking
about relationships, what's good about them,
what's bad, and how each relationship
is unique – god! he hates that word, *relationship*,
and she knows it, knows he talks like that
when he isn't saying what he means. She flips off
the covers and slides out of bed. It's a queen-sized mattress.
He'd been arguing for a king as if this one isn't big enough –
the bottom sheet an ice floe stretching between them –
and alone, she at the dresser now, he knows he's drifting
into a chilled and open space. In front of the mirror
she turns on the lamp – bad sign, she's slipped into

her nightgown – and sits on the round padded stool she found
at a vintage shop, the previous owner a minor actress.
"And I am made more beautiful by losses," she says,
quoting something he's forgotten, dipping two fingers
into a squat white jar and smearing cold cream on her cheeks.

METEOROLOGY

The weather can't make up its mind. Clouds above the city
spiral in and stall, then double back. It's her own discord
she's walking into. The wind in her hair is from the north;
it chills her thinking, her good intent. She's as cold as a star;
inside her chest, snow is falling. It melts, then freezes, her lungs
fish trapped in ice. The others on the street slap by in sandals,
skin sizzling in the sun. She's in sandals too, and her dress
is cotton and July. The winter of my discontent –
how little she remembers from those years of study,
the poetry of unhappiness so apropos, exact,
though weren't those words about a war about to happen,
not a woman's small betrayal? The dogs distract her,
a boxer with sunglasses and beret, a tall grey poodle,
under the stubble his newly exposed skin
the blue of bruises. She is trying to love the world so much
she'll love her husband. The wind changes its direction,
drags her down the crowded street toward the man
who waits for her nine storeys above the trees, his white shirt
immaculate, his trousers pressed. The sky digresses.
A priest in robe and running shoes shouts to no one
she can see, *No, no, no*, then, *I don't want you anymore.*
Can that be right? Too old for babies, a woman pushes
a buggy and won't give way. It's full of stones, a sign
pinned to the canopy meant to shade says *Clocks For Sale.*
Conceptual or mad? A hundred stones are ticking.
Above the upper limits cirrus thin into manes and tails,
the rest of the mares invisible – such things
predict a change. Finally, the falafel stand and the long breads
of Paris tucked into a basket in the bakery doorway
fill her nostrils with a longing for somewhere else, a simple

goodness, a necessary lie, an assignation à la Aphra Behn
that might save a country or, at least, a life. At last she's through
the doors and in the lobby: Antarctic chandelier, a rug whose
    plushness
registers her tracks. The desk clerk, barely older than her son,
gold crest above the pocket of his jacket that's too big
across the shoulders, turns his face away (do they teach this
in hotel school?) as she weathers past him to the stairwell
in her dress of falling rain.

THE RIPEST BERRIES ARE NOT WHOLE

Grey shadow inside the thick rasp-
berry thatch, a cane bends
with the weight of something
denser than a bird,
and she jumps back, her pail
spilling. It's the whole
berries she's kept, the torn
she's picked and eaten –
guessing they'd been pecked
by robins, their breasts stained.

Now she's sure it's rats.
For days she has swallowed
the spit of rats. She tries not

to panic. Tries to think
of something to balance
this disgust. Naked forefeet
holding the berry
with such finesse it stays
on the stem, small teeth
nibbling and leaving half
as if around a crowded table
the rat had learned to share.

Perhaps its spit will give the gift
of prophecy, the taste of rat
in her mouth
a new kind of speaking,
without beauty,
without guile.

THE END OF SWALLOWS

Did he hear it right? Was he awake or in some tired dream?
She beside him in their bed: "I don't love you anymore."
Could there be worse? A stranger on the phone, a call
about a child, a doctor's voice – that single word
tossing him like a sack into a gorge he can't climb out of.
He listens to her breathing. Steady, deep, surely
she's asleep. He turns his head. The numbers count in red
3:00, then 3:01. The cat door flaps, and spiralling up the stairs
a yowl that means a kill, some rat or baby rabbit twitching
on the rug, his turn to clean it up. They love this cat,
praise him for rodents but not a bird. The white hair under his chin
bright with blood. That was yesterday. Nothing left
but the bile duct and a naked tail curved like a comma
suggesting more to come and it's arrived. 3:05.
The new duvet is silk: the cover stitched with swallows in a dive.
The birds are dying out. It's the pesticides, the mono-crops
too bold, too yellow for the eye to hold. As a child he got a dime
a nest to knock them off the walls of the garage,
mud shattering at his feet, shards of pottery from a ruin.
He's made of stone. Afraid to move, he could be lying on a slab
with a spaniel on his feet. Did she speak? Is she practising
for morning, thinking he can't hear? He has to keep the cat
off the silk. The sharpness of his claws unravels
the swallows made of thread. They're dying out.
Isn't that the worst? Should he say it first?
I don't love you anymore. The heart kicked open, hinges
snapped, and he can't step back, he must
by himself walk through.

CROW'S TAKE ON MAN

More rapacious than us, more needy.
They never take the shortest route
and use too many words when a caw would do.
Their hearts work like ours, but theirs are bitter
in our beaks. Even snow can't take away the taste.
They're too simple to grasp there is an end to everything.
They don't know their shadows have blood in them.
They don't know their souls build nests of sticks
to hold the shiny things they can't get by without.
O, what the marrow of the wind could teach them,
the river's gizzard, the deer's blue lips and tongue.
Until they're ready, we won't let them
hear our songs.

MORE LAST QUESTIONS
(after W.S. Merwin)

What is the grass?
    The lost ones, talking.

What is the forest?
    Light's tall coffins.

What is the ocean?
    An ancient book of blues
the whales leave behind.

What is the tongue?
    Nobody speaks under the snow.

No, what is the tongue?
    Heel of snake, thumb of earthworm.

No, what is the tongue?

The moon, caught in a trap,
    chews off its right leg
then its left
              so it can rise.

THE WRONG CAT

The artist, slipping bobby pins into her thinning hair
as if to knot it at the back cleared her thinking, said,
"Help me find a title," and they, husband and wife,
stared more intently at the swirls of red and blue
and that darker colour where they met. The wife said,
"The Naked Novelist," and they laughed as they'd laughed
earlier at dinner, the man confessing, except for socks,
as he pushed his stories to their end, he dressed only
when the inspiration or, more accurately, the cold
moved him. The wife, who was a writer too, a poet,
knew he'd told this lie so the artist would imagine him
naked on his swivel chair, so she'd capture with
her eye and brush the light from the screen, the same kind
that falls from a fridge, casting its chill across his chest,
the vulnerability of his belly, a harmless fib, after all,
a small flirtation between good friends and not all of him,
his wife would like to add, a pretty picture.
Over the last of the wine, the three had searched
in a close-to-drunken haze for the surname of the author
whose wife locked him in a room without clothes or food
until he finished another chapter. Russian, they agreed, it sounds
like a Russian writer's wife. The woman, not the artist
but the poet, kept gazing at that purple-black on the canvas,
how charged, how kinetic. If she looked away, would it blast
through the walls and deep into the night? "Infinity's
Origami," she said, the artist making a *hmmm*
of appreciation or a polite I-don't-think-so. The poet argued
for infinity's deft fingers in the cold of outer space
folding the darkness into shape after shape, killing time.
The husband, who'd been quiet, stumped, both women thought,

said, "The Wrong Cat," and for no reason she could understand
his wife knew it was exactly right and said so. In the end
the artist chose infinity over cat. Maybe that's why the painting,
though chosen for shows over several years, never sold.
The wife, poet that she was, couldn't stop thinking of his title,
so odd and apt. It brought the evening back, the stories
they passed around the table, their laughter candlelit,
their sadness too. He'd talked of his first wife, both nineteen
when they'd wed, both useless around the house. She'd
collected cats; ten or so snaked their way among the small legs
of the children, two daughters and a son, under four. It was before
he'd become good enough – or should he say, *connected* enough –
to teach or get a decent grant. He worked as a gas jockey,
a clerk in a menswear store, the driver of a butcher's van, blood
from a Francis Bacon still life soaking through the brown paper
if he wasn't fast enough. On hot days the house they rented
stank from the attic insulation the cats used as litter.
When they made love, that's what he smelled in her hair.
After he'd left, after she'd told him she'd slept with all his friends,
she claimed she just wanted to be happy. "How could she be
    happy?"
he asked that night, more wax on the tablecloth than under the
    flames.
No one was happy then. Not the kids, not him, not the cats.

IV

A cat can walk on snow
without breaking
through; it can walk on clouds.
If you follow its trails
for a day in the garden,
your feet will grow lighter.
By night you'll be walking
on your dreams.
This is the first lesson
in flying without wings.

A DISTURBANCE OF FLIES

[An older man and woman at a kitchen table, the signs of a finished
breakfast around them. Both are reading the newspaper.]
So what do a watch and a ruler have in common?
I don't know, he says.
Then you're off to a nursing home. It's one of the questions
       on a test for Alzheimer's.
I thought it was a joke, like knock, knock, who's there,
       that's why I said I don't know.
Well, now that you're aware it's not a joke, answer the question.
They both measure something, he says.
That's what I said too. Do you think we got it right?
If we didn't, we'll both go to the home together.
[He leaves the kitchen. She hears a whack!
whack! whack! coming from the living room.
He's at the window, a rolled-up newspaper in his hand.]
What are you doing? she asks.
I'm on fly patrol. I killed about fifty yesterday.
Fifty? Where are they coming from? It's January.
They're coming from inside.
That means there's something dead in here.
They're odd flies too, he says. Slow and stupid.
       It's easy to swat them.
Could they have come from a mouse that died behind the bookcase?
They don't buzz either.
Are you wearing your hearing aid? . . . No, you're right. I don't hear
   them.
There's something creepy about a silent fly.
There's something creepy about a watch and a ruler. I bet a lot
   of perfectly

sound people couldn't answer that question.
What do flies and a watch have in common? he asks.
What about a ruler and a row of dead flies? I can see them
as inch marks, can't you?
The trick is they all measure something even if we can't remember
what it is.

LATE DIALOGUE

If, he says.
      If what? she asks.

If fish, if death.
      Whose? she asks.

If bird, if storm, if fire.
      Where?

If you, if me, if Tuesday –
           – if Tuesday?

        If fist, he says, if meat,
if wasp, if blunt, if shovel, if want, if want.

She takes off his glasses.
Kisses his high forehead.
Dips her finger in brandy and runs it along
his lower lip. If yes, she says,
if do.

BETWEEN DOG AND WOLF

There's an hour at dusk when a wolf may be mistaken for a dog.
Which one – gaunt and ravenous – will you choose to call,
open your door to, and let in? A man may be mistaken
for a pine, dwarfed by cold, branches stripped.
Either way, that figure standing on the rise
could warm your house, could find a place to burn.
Entre le chien et le loup. You say out loud the words
this hour is known by. Such a narrow space
between a name and nothing. Between fear and who
you fear you are. Dog, tree, man, wolf: a woman can be
mistaken for. As the day leans further into darkness,
you're sure it's just the wind, out of sorts,
un-witted, skulking around your door.

BLACKBERRY PICKERS

This is the hour of the blackberry pickers,
before the birds bring in the dawn,
before the smell of coffee wafts from the window
of the farmhouse across the road. The quail
have nipped the lower berries, deer have eaten
those waist-high. Though no one has seen them
the blackberry pickers must stand on stools,
on ladders, on one another's shoulders, arms gloved
from fingertip to elbow, heads wrapped in scarves.

Is it chance that brings them here the exact moment
the black deepens into sweetness? Is it greed
that clears the branches, leaves nothing
for the woman who walks early morning from her door
with just an ice-cream bucket to pick enough for a pie?
If there were gypsies in these parts, they'd be blamed.
If there were refugees, if there were wild children.

Cars coasting, headlights snuffed, they come noiseless
in the dark and in the dark they vanish,
before the cats want in, before the barn owl roosts
above the sleeping horses, before raccoons gather
their little ones and climb the ancient fir, pulling
themselves higher branch by branch
with fingers deft enough to etch a greeting
on a grain of rice, flick salt from a bag of pepper,
pluck pennies from the eyelids of the newly dead.

MOOSE NOSE

It's the most orbicular,
the biggest nose

of our country's ungulates,
mimicking, as much as anything,

a crook-necked squash, the one
that won the ribbon at the country fair.

❖

The moose is so powerful
his singular is plural,

yet when you come upon him
at the edge of the forest,

his nose relaxes you. It makes you laugh.
It's as if the craftsman assigned to the task

had never made a nose before,
as if the moose was his first try,

and after that, he was demoted to construct
the scrotum of the sea lion,

the toenail on the *Homo sapiens'*
big toe.

❖

It's so risible, so homely, we call
the biggest, thickest tight end

on the football team Moose,
though, in truth, he studies poetry

at NYU and John Ashbery
chose him as his only undergrad.

❧

If you're still chuckling – schnozzle,
conk, bulbous bazoom – take another look

at the beast you've come upon
who is looking at you,

who is thinking.

A great tree grows out of his head,
a tree where no birds rest

and the wind, though it can smash
a granary into the ground

and levitate a tractor from field to field,
can't budge the branches.

Moreover, the tree is rooted
in the moose's mind,

a northern mind, a swamp mind,
a mind of huge imaginings,

so complex
Samuel Beckett and Virginia Woolf

wait in line at dusk for his office hours
so they can have a chat.

TOBIAS'S DOG AND THE ANGEL

It's hard to believe no one knew
Raphael was an angel. Robed,
feet dusty from the road he travelled
with Tobias and a small white dog,
he still had a glow about him
most evident when he didn't know
anyone was looking and he forgot to pull
his radiance inside.

Sometimes the glory of the earth
was too much for him. He could stare for hours
at the slimness of a lily's throat, wonder at the wit
and perfection of the wren, fall into rapture
when the dog licked his ear.

When it was time to go, he left Tobias
but tucked the dog against his chest and rose.
The other six who stood fiery at God's side
delighted in the darkness of the canine eye,
his affability, the freckled, almost naked belly
that even Gabriel, who bowed to no one,
bent down to kiss. He was the angel
who had to hold his breath because
his trumpet note would spell the end of things.

Even God, who'd lost track of much
of what he'd fashioned,
when he saw the dog, said, *Let him stay.*
Thus began the rising of the animals;
singly or in a herd, dreamy, not knowing
what path they travelled, ahead of them
the sound of Tobias's dog barking at the gate.

OWL'S TAKE ON MAN

We know more
about their god than they do.
They can't hear his silence
as he drops on hungry wings
into the world.

They can't see him in the dark
when he moves among us,
when he collects our pellets
among the fallen leaves
and takes them apart,

spits on the little bones
to clean them,
and one by one,
reconstructs the mice.

MY MOTHER LIES DYING

Sunshine after
days of rain. A wren
hangs its shadow
on the fence to dry.

What a risk it's taking!
I need a swatch of darkness
to sew a pocket
to hold her final breath.

OLD STYLE

Count the crows, my father said,
on the Old Style Pilsner label,
then the rabbits. One, two, three –
I loved the beer smell of his breath
as he whisker-rubbed my cheeks – four!
Oh, you're the clever one, he said.

There were also Indians, a red jalopy,
a biplane with a rabbit in the pilot's seat,
and a train, grey smudge above its smokestack.
These days, I ride it to get back, press my cheek
against the glass, watch everything slip by so fast.

Tonight it's winter, the train's unheated.
The bottle's frosted around the lip
as if sipped by moonlight. Up ahead
I glimpse a man at a station, boarded-up.

He's small enough to be my father
standing there, swinging a lantern
against the cold, snow falling all around him
so I can barely see. The train won't stop.
Count the crows, he said, and I count them still.

DEER'S TAKE ON MAN

We come upon them
at the edge of the clearing,
camouflaged by leaves, the wind
blowing their stench behind them.
The dark parts of them pour out
streams of light. Once we sense them,
it's too late. Some have an eye
deadly and quick, it burns through the air
and our blood pulls us down.

There are others who give us something else.
Their look is a kind of touching. It strokes
our mouths, rubs the velvet on our antlers.
There's a sadness to them then.
It's as if they want to crawl inside
and live between the cages of our ribs.

They don't know the trees are seeing them,
they don't know the snow is seeing them,
they don't know the grass is a kindness
their flesh has given to the earth.

THE PONY

"I want a pony to take me home," she said
and though she meant she was tired of walking,
and he understood – the light almost gone, the road dusty,
horseflies banging into their arms and faces
like doughy pebbles – something nameless caught
on the breeze and chilled his skin. It was death's pony,
he knew it, and already he could sense its coming, hooves
falling on the summer grasses, nostrils flaring, his wife's scent
drawing it toward them. Was the pony raised for this purpose only,
never put to work until this moment, like the white horses the old
    Saxons
kept in a grove for divination? The way one grazed, ducked its head
or pulled the reins displaying what was to come to the village
and from which direction. They kept walking, he held
her arm lightly, not wanting her to startle or notice his unease.
Was that a flash of its mane ahead, just below the clouds
where the sun stalled in its sinking? That chill again, and an ache
so deep inside he stumbled, no, no, no! If he clapped his hands,
if he shouted . . . "The flies?" she asked. Then delighting
in her foolishness, her little girl's wish, she smiled at him.
"I'll ride it bareback," she said. "And we'll go so fast
I'll have supper ready for you when you get home."

ACKNOWLEDGEMENTS

The title "An Extraordinary Fondness for Beetles" is a play on the title *An Inordinate Fondness for Beetles* by Arthur V. Evans and Charles L. Bellamy. If you have an interest in these insects, I highly recommend their book. The title "Not Troubled by Her Breath" is the last phrase of number VIII of Rilke's *Sonnets to Orpheus*. The quotation at the end of "The Question" is from Howard Moss's poem "The Pruned Tree."

I'm grateful to the editors of the following publications in which these poems appeared: *The Malahat Review, Herstory, University of Toronto Quarterly, The Fiddlehead, Best Canadian Poetry 2013, Nimrod, Grain, Vallum,* and *Sitelines: Landscape Architecture in British Columbia.* The series "Man from Elsewhere" was first published in 2013 as a limited-edition chapbook by Jack Pine Press. The cat poems that introduce each section were translated into Spanish by Carmen Leñero and first published in *La Perspectiva del Gato* by Trilce Ediciones in Mexico City in 2009. Many thanks to Carmen for making this Spanish edition of my poetry possible.

Donna Bennett has been my editor since 1985, when I first published with McClelland & Stewart. How blessed I am for her brilliance and support and for her esoteric knowledge of the creatures of the earth. I'd like to thank Ellen Seligman for her belief in poetry, Anita Chong for her care and her meticulous attention to all of my queries, Heather Sangster for her excellent eye, and Russell Thorburn, who helped me shape an early version of the manuscript. Patrick Lane has meant everything to me – he's my first reader, best friend, muse, and husband. We grow old together in the garden he has made for us.